Jealo

How To Overcome Jealousy, Insecurity and Trust Issues Save Your Relationship, Love Life and Emotions

By

Sofia Price

Table of Contents

Introduction

I want to thank you and congratulate you for buying the book, "Jealousy: How to Overcome Jealousy, Insecurity and Trust Issues - Save Your Relationship, Love Life and Emotions"

This book contains proven steps and strategies on how to deal with your jealousy and ultimately save your relationship from falling prey into this green-eyed monstrosity. It's a state of mind that holds you back from your full potential and is something that you really do need to deal with.

Addressing your jealousy is vital to the health of every relationship that you have, whether with friends or lovers. Overcoming it, including addressing your trust and insecurity issues, makes you a better person at the end of the day. That better person will be able to forge relationships that give him/her confidence so that jealousy is not needed. This green eyed monster kills relationships and takes away the potential of a relationship ever being a fulfilling experience. Stem it now before it's too late because, when you do, you will find you can meet people on equal terms and that's what real relationship making is all about.

Although you may think that jealousy is only temporary and doesn't really bother you too much, if you have let it into your life already, it's starting to eat away at the person that you are. You need to stem it before it becomes an obsession. When it does, your life becomes a hell and will certainly drive people you love away from you. Why? Read on and you will find out. It's probably the best investment you have ever made in your life. The book is written by an expert in the field who learned, from personal experience, that the green eyed monster only holds you back. It can never make things within your life fulfilling. The base problem that causes jealousy needs to be faced head on, and that's where I am here to help you.

Thanks again for buying this book, I hope you enjoy it but, more than that, I hope you gain a little insight into why you feel jealousy and are able to stop that green monster in its tracks. Once you do, life becomes a much nicer place and you attract the kind of people you want to attract, without frightening them away by displaying your insecurities.

Chapter 1 – Jealousy is a Warning: Something within You Needs Attention

It's what fuels the suspense in your favorite novels; authors often use it as a motive for murder. It even comes with its own color.

Jealousy – that green-eyed monster (Shakespeare called it that) is always lurking behind us, always readying itself to strike. It sets up camp at the top of your head while in a relationship, and it glows with such malice as you grow deeply and madly in love with your partner, and as you are becoming comfortably attached as well. This also happens even when you are not in the mood to like your partner in particular situations.

Your sweetheart may have called you by someone else's name, or you found out how his eyes lingered on your best friend for too long. Sometimes, he talks excitedly about some girl at work. And long before you know it, you're on fire already. And the fire spreads through that sickening combination of suspicion, possessiveness, rage, humiliation, and ultimately, your insecurity.

Neither gender can be routinely full of those jealous feelings, although women tend to go the extra mile just to win back their lovers. Men, on the other hand, rely more on their status and money, flaunting them as they go, normally walking out of relationships to save face and protect their self-esteem.

Taming jealousy is never easy, but you can manage it, and that's what's important.

Everyone knows how it feels to be jealous of someone else. Jealousy, among other traits that define human feelings, could readily be among the most harmful emotions that we display. Think of it as that nagging belief of inferiority/spite to another person, mostly due to mutual interests. It's only normal that we human beings ooze and smell of jealousy at the right moments. And insecurity is not far behind. In fact, jealousy features heavily in our insecurities in our relationships.

Why Do We Have Insecurities and Trust Issues in Our Relationships?

Some people keep on asking themselves why, at some point in their lives, they experience insecurity and trust issues in their relationships. This most troublesome issue manifests when our partners have not done anything wrong, or anything to make us sad, and yet here we are' our ears are red hot with jealousy.

What we must understand is that we project our jealousy in different ways, like when there is just cause, or any other reasons to make us jealous. This could be a classic case where the partner has done some things that are suspicious at the least.

We also need to see from another angle if all circumstances indicate that we are actually the ones controlling our relationships and not the other way around, or whether our partners are projecting jealousy instead.

Do you feel insecure in your current relationship, often leaving you lonely, worried, and ultimately jealous? Do you hear your partner say that you can be "clingy" at times? It could well be that you're having an anxious attachment. It's a way of describing how individuals connect to one another, especially to their 'emotionally significant'. Individuals experiencing anxious attachment think they're flawed, and that they're unworthy of love.

Our sense of attachment, believe it or not, starts to develop during infancy. In some cases, infants came to know their parents were inconsistently available. This distressed them along the way, which their parents then addressed by giving them extra attention. As they grow up, these kids could also receive attention from others.

And over time, they start to develop that 'needy feeling', desperate for attention, including the need for other individuals to help soothe them. Kids with anxious attachment grow up believing they have to earn the attention and support of others just because they are flawed. Such beliefs naturally affect their relationships. They often become self-critical, questioning themselves regularly. This can be tiring to their loved ones and friends who support them.

All this means they also cling to their relationships with other individuals, and they can easily get jealous as well.

Fortunately, anxious attachment is never permanent. With self-compassion and awareness, you can build and nurture healthy relationships.

Unprovoked Jealousy is Bad News

Even if it feels justified at the time, unprovoked jealousy only creates marital issues that suggest how one side is controlling the other. Why could you be acting this way? Consider these possibilities:

- You might tend to pick on someone who's acting provocatively. If this indeed happened, did you ever get an overdose of provocative behavior coming from your parents?

- It could be that you question your value to others. Have you ever thought why your partner picked you over hotter girls out there or girls who are more fun?

- It may also be that you are clamoring for drama in your life. Are you looking for excitement to make it all worthwhile, to help you see yourself as valuable?

- Maybe you have yet to consider if closeness scares you. If this is the case, do you see yourself maintaining your distance from fully committing to a relationship? This is where jealousy could come into the picture as a way of setting boundaries in relationships.

- Ultimately, you justify your jealousy to support your true love feelings.

Note that all this means your jealousy is rooted deep in your own issues. If all these possibilities describe you, then take time for some introspection. Change how you look at yourself. How you talk to yourself should stand against ideas that justify your jealousy. Jealousy is about as negative as you can get and that won't ever work in your favor. Perhaps you have seen teens use jealousy to tempt some lost love back on track, but it reality it doesn't work. It shows immaturity and insecurity and that's bad news as far as a new love or even an old one is concerned.

Getting Past Your Insecurities

While you could work on this issue on your own, in some cases you won't have to. Psychotherapy may save the day, either as a couple, or mainly on your own. Even if it's an individual issue in your case, it still impacts your relationship. What you need to do is explore your insecurities and work out why you have them. If you want to do this and are close enough to your partner to ask his/her help, then it's quite possible that your partner will take this as a great compliment. We don't let many people into our private bubble of thoughts and sometimes a partner is happy to work through your issues because at the end of the day, it makes your relationship stronger and it helps you to understand each other.

Look at events in the past that made you feel so bad. Have you been let down? Have you been so badly hurt by an event that you are letting it hold you back in your current lifestyle? The fact is that often jealousy comes out of seeing a similar situation occur or actually perceiving that it will occur. Your last partner told you that he was working late. You found out that he was having an affair. You now see problems arising when your new partner tells you that he is working late.

He needs to know why you are feeling insecure and when he does, he will help you get beyond jealousy. If you don't discuss it, how will he know what he is doing wrong or that your point of view tells you that he is? You also need to look at self-esteem issues. Are you always asking for extra attention? Do you constantly ask him if he loves you? These are signs of insecurity and to be honest, are not very endearing ones. You should know you are loved. You should know that you don't need extra attention, but some people do because issues from the past tell them that they do. It's actually very off-putting in a relationship to show so little trust and a relationship based upon insecurity is doomed from the word "go."

If you have an insecurity, talk about it. Let your partner know the kind of things that happened to you in your past early in the relationship. When you feel jealous because of something such as this, remind him of your insecurities and talk about it. Let your partner know, above all else, that you know it's unreasonable to feel jealous but that part of you won't let you let go. Ask for his help. Often people like to protect their partners and if they are aware that there is a past issue may be open to being understanding when a situation arises.

If you are really having problems getting past issues from your past, then perhaps talking to a professional will help, but do let your partner know. Your partner will be more sympathetic toward you and behave in a way that he knows won't hurt you, but you do need to get jealousy out of your system. It's unhealthy and it may be stopping you from living life to the full.

Examine your motives. Examine your reasoning and try to replace jealousy with something more constructive. If you find yourself becoming suspicious, try to think about something else. The problem is that you are potentially leading yourself up the garden path by being jealous.

The reason I say this is because when you do what you are doing, you put all chances of good things happening out of reach. If you're jealous, you don't get what you want out of life. You never can because you cannot control people. You need to know that the problem isn't the people around you, but the way that you react toward the people and their behavior. You cannot continually blame someone else for your jealous responses. That's down to you and if you really need help with this problem do seek out the help of a professional to try and get you beyond it.

Let's look at the negative effects of jealousy:

1. It makes you less of a person, not more of one.

2. It alienates people you love and who love you.

3. It makes you look insecure and sometimes foolish.

4. It makes you say things that you may regret.

The future chapters give you a lot of detail about jealousy and ways to overcome that horrible feeling that you get when you allow jealousy to become part of your life. It's never worth it. If he is going to leave you, being jealous won't stop him. If he's going through a bad patch and needs your support, jealous behavior may just be enough to drive him away.

Think about it. You need to handle your feelings better and put jealousy where it belongs – deep in the past. You have decided to go forward in life and when you can put jealousy into the past, your life becomes a much happier place to be. It also becomes a much more pleasurable place for him to be and if that's what you are aiming for, it's your only alternative.

The problem is that people see jealousy as the negative response that it is. Men tend to back away from it. Women tend to be flattered initially by it, but locked into relationships that do not satisfy them when their man shows jealousy. No one gains at all. The green eyed monster is not becoming. It doesn't make you look vulnerable in a nice kind of way. It makes you look insecure and stubborn to the point that you make the people you love suffer. Now, that's time to stop and take a good look at what you are doing because if you don't you will lose them.

Jealousy is one of the most negative feelings that a person can have and erodes a relationship which is supposed to be built on trust. You need to put that trust to the test now and tell your loved one what's bugging you and why, rather than harboring jealous thoughts. In fact, you need to find a way around it that does not demonstrate jealousy at all, but instead a reasonable explanation of why you are feeling negative. Remember, it's your feelings that are being bounced around but remember also that it's usually self-inflicted and you need to get past it.

In the chapters that follow, you will see where jealousy stems from and decide how to move forward. Unless you are willing to do this, don't be surprised if you lose friends and lose the very person that you fear losing, as a direct result of your jealous behavior. It's unacceptable behavior in a trusting relationship and when the trust is gone, the relationship isn't based upon a solid footing any more.

Chapter 2 – Where Your Jealousy Comes From

Jealousy in relationships and marriage is very real. And it destroys. Fortunately, we can all do something about it and become a better partner at the end of the day. Is your jealousy called for? Are there good reasons why you should be jealous and insecure?

If it happens that jealousy is a new feeling in your current relationship, something must be going on. This is especially true whenever you do not understand where that jealous feeling comes from, leaving you confused and angry.

One of the most logical reasons behind it is how you are not feeling good enough about who you are. This feeling of jealousy is most probably a projection—you are jealous of a certain characteristic or trait that has yet to identify you. At the same time, you could have been drawn to your partner's confidence.

The fact is that jealousy doesn't just happen. It happens because of an underlying problem and you need to find out what that problem is. This is vital to actually getting beyond it. It will also be prompted by certain triggers and you need to know what these are. It would be a good idea to write down a list of the reasons why you believe that you are jealous, together with your line of thinking and past experiences. This may help you to make sense of it all and it's better that you try to work this out yourself at this stage of the game, rather than reveal all of your feelings which may well be unjustified, and as a result of how you are feeling due to a temporary situation.

Think Before You Act

If you can readily identify specific behaviors of your partner that instigated your insecurity, you should talk your concerns over with your partner first. Understand that how you express such concerns could help improve the relationship afterwards, or harm it. Criticism doesn't help anyone. Typical criticism could include:

- You go out too much without me

- You have everything and I've got nothing

- I can't handle being alone all the time and you don't give me enough time

These are very negative ways to deal with jealousy. They won't work because when a partner feels criticized, you are questioning his/her way of dealing with things and constricting them. People who feel pushed around will leave because it's the only choice left open to them. Try talking it through, using these phrases instead of the above phrases:

- I miss you when you're gone, but I'll be here when you get back

- You're a wonderful person and maybe we can be wonderful together

- I have a little bit of a problem that I need you to help me with. I'm not that good with being alone.

You put over to your partner that none of this is his/her fault and you get a better response. A man who feels that he will return to a nagging woman because he has been out too long won't actually look forward to going back to her. A man who feels that his woman is waiting for him and is thinking positive thoughts about him will be more likely to want to go back to her. However, if you do have psychological problems with being alone, then you do need to discuss these without criticizing your partner and making it his/her fault. By enlisting your partner's help, you may be able to come up with solutions that help you through the day. I know one of my partners helped me with my insecurity but had I approached in a negative manner, I would have killed the relationship dead.

It is also vital that you are able to discuss your concerns and feelings without even accusing your partner. If you start by lashing out accusations, your partner will automatically be on the offensive. Worse, you'll end up in a jealousy-based relationship, which only creates chaos. And you wouldn't want that.

The thing that you need to remember is that woman are made up of emotions. Men, however, are made in a different way. If you are a woman and have jealousy issues and put them over as being your insecurities rather than his, he will do what he can to protect you. If you are a man and you have jealousy in your mind, you will drive your woman away if you try and voice this in a way that makes her feel like she isn't doing enough to keep the relationship together. Either way, personal criticism doesn't help anyone – least of all you.

The Art of Bringing Your Jealousy and Insecurity Out Into the Open

Before you can approach your partner, teach yourself first how you will begin the conversation USING AN OPEN MIND! Tell yourself that you are simply going to talk to your friend, and not someone else. Go with the possibility that you may have just misunderstood the situation, or that what you have is incorrect information, and that you would want to correct and close the case. This makes you positive in your approach. It also helps greatly not to apportion blame. Negative things such as blame tend to alienate people and it won't help your cause. This is YOUR problem, not theirs and you need them to help you to deal with your problem, not change their lives to adjust to your problem. That's unreasonable.

Giving Him/Her the Benefit of the Doubt

Learn to give him/her the benefit of the doubt as well. This is very helpful. Trust in your partner that, whenever something happens, it is not his/her intention to cause bad feeling. Trust that he/she doesn't want to hurt you.

The point is we normally conclude that we are unloved, unimportant, or worse, controlled whenever we are hurt. We tend to forget that this is only a feeling, and not reality. We forget that the evidence is there. Your partner is entitled to the benefit of the doubt since everything begins with the belief that he does not intend to hurt you during the course of your relationship. Their actions could be down to stress and fatigue at work, their own habits and needs, and many more reasons.

Try it, and you'll see how it makes a difference. It's how everyone gets around not sweating all the small stuff. The problem is that the small stuff gets exaggerated by your mind and you need to recognize the difference between your perception and the reality.

Ask yourself:

- Why am I jealous?

- Did my partner really give me reason to be?

- Is it through a past experience with someone else?

The point is that people often feel jealousy because of their own insecurity rather than the guilty actions of their partner. Your partner looks in the direction of someone prettier than you – you feel upset. What you should be feeling is flattered that he's with you. In the case of a man – If men are ogling your lady, then be flattered and make her feel special, rather than letting your own insecurities make her feel like she did anything wrong.

Which leads us to relationship boundaries and their importance to the health and growth of relationships. If your partner is already close to, or has already crossed, that boundary set by your relationship, you have to become specific about any expectations on the boundaries set by your relationship. To do this successfully you have to ask your partner for his input on this matter. Again, you'll get better results if you go for a friendly-atmosphere approach, rather than confront him head on in a full steam ahead manner. Maybe you are misreading a situation and you won't make such a fool of yourself if you approach it in a gentle manner, rather than throwing blame your partner's way.

Chapter 3 - Creating Relationship Boundaries to Address Jealousy

This chapter generally talks about the need to create realistic expectations in every relationship to keep jealousy at bay. As you already know, jealousy really wreaks havoc in relationships. There may be good causes for jealousy in certain situations, but at other times, fears and insecurity pave the way for those jealous feelings. Experts agree that setting up relationship boundaries is a good way to ease down on those jealous feelings. Whether justified or not, jealous feelings will gain you absolutely nothing at all. In fact, they make you look immature and foolish in the eyes of your beloved. Perhaps if your beloved has erred, jealousy will only make them feel guilty for a short time. It isn't something you should entertain long term, as they are even more likely to stray again. The reason? Your partner can only take a certain amount of criticism. If you think of a child that has done something wrong, you can't keep ramming it down their throats without having some kind of impact on the child. Similarly, once you have forgiven, you can't keep bringing up jealous issues because if you do, you may just as well have finished the relationship and it may not be worthwhile saving.

The Importance of Relationship Boundaries

Both you and your partner must positively set relationship boundaries to define realistic expectations for partner behavior. Through such boundaries, both sides will know what instances could make each one jealous, and can then move on to avoid going off-limits, or the mere thought of going off-limits.

It pays to know the specifics of the boundaries. If not, you guys will not achieve concise and realistic expectations in the relationship. Dealing more with the specifics makes it easier to translate those that are 'not allowed'. As you set up the boundaries, meeting halfway could be a challenge. One side may declare that full-boy hugging or flirting is within the accepted limits for example, and the other fully wants to dump such ideas outside the boundary. This is where things could get a bit rough. You have to prepare for this.

Consider these as your relationship's fail-safe boundaries. These are, without a doubt, over the limit. Both of you need to highlight and reference them to reduce cases of future arguing.

It would be smart to identify the so-called 'safer positions' in every relationship. After having considered the fail-safe boundaries, how do you propose to put your relationship in a safer position? Following the given example, if both sides agreed that full body hugs would already be going over the line, a much safer position would be those one-armed, side-by-side hugs. To make it even safer, better propose no more hugging with anyone of the opposite sex instead. This would undoubtedly be one very clear boundary.

This is so since you value your relationship, and you would go to lengths to care for and protect it, especially from potential danger.

Make a Commitment

Commit yourself to follow the set boundaries. It may be necessary to modify them along the way; you need a stable fence around your relationship to help remind both of you of the value of the relationship and having each other despite the odds. It also helps both of you to get a good grip of this long-term investment. Once you are both working toward the same boundaries and understand each other's point of view, you really can work out problems when lines are overstepped, without letting the jealousy monster out of the bag. Make a commitment to your partner and to yourself that these boundaries will take away any chance of jealousy creeping in.

It's actually easier to make this kind of commitment in a marriage situation because you have made vows which you expect to be kept. These act as great boundaries, but if you are unmarried, you have not yet made these vows. Thus, you need to outline what is and what is not acceptable to you. For example:

Unfaithfulness is not permitted

There will be an agreed amount of time spent together

The first is an obvious boundary. If you are seriously committed to each other, it's reasonable to expect exclusivity, especially since disease is so rife these days. The second consideration means that you expect your partner to give you a reasonable amount of his/her time and that you can both have a certain amount of time for other friendships. It's important within a relationships that friendships continue. Romances should never be exclusive of family commitments and time for friends.

Putting Jealousy behind You

If you are able to go through the steps shown in this chapter, then you are acknowledging that there is a problem and dealing with it, rather than letting it lurk in the background of your relationship. Imagine each jealous action as a prod with a sharp object because there are only so many prods that someone can endure and if you persist on continual jealousy, the only way that this will lead is to the end of the relationship. Put it behind you firmly and if you find it trying to escape its box, slam the lid.

Jealousy really is counter-productive to happiness. It will eat away at who you are and who other people see you as being. It's not a nice way to be. In fact, if you know people who are overly jealous, can you really say that you agree with the way that they treat each other? It's very unlikely because jealousy erodes any relationship even one that starts off as a very strong one indeed. When jealousy gets introduced, the relationship grinds to a halt because the trust is gone and no relationship can exist without that trust element.

Knowing how to stop jealousy in its tracks

What people generally find is that jealousy is a temporary state of mind caused by insecurity. If a woman believes that she isn't good enough for her man, she will doubt his motives for staying. She will obsess about it and if he decides to go out or work late, she will immediately assume that he's doing it so that he doesn't have to spend time with her. The problem with this vicious circle is that the more she obsesses and the less self-esteem she has, the less he really will want to be with her. Ask yourself, would you want to be with someone that:

- Needed to know your whereabouts at all times?

- Checks up on you when you go somewhere?

- Obsesses about the amount of time you spend away from home?

I know I would feel extremely uncomfortable if my partner started to display any of these behaviors. Why? Because in our relationship, we have an element of trust. If he wants to vacation on his own, I think that's a great idea because it also gives me a little time on my own to do my own thing. Imagine if I said "no" and put limitations on him that are unreasonable. That's what you do whenever you exhibit jealousy.

To stop jealousy in its tracks, imagine how much nicer it would be to replace it with trust. Begin to like yourself. Begin to feel yourself worthy because you are. Everyone is until they display behavior which is unacceptable and which questions trust. Jealousy is the first rate way to kill your relationship. If you are broken, **fix you**. Then jealousy won't happen anymore. If your partner isn't worth trusting, he isn't worth holding onto. Close the relationship and start to enjoy being you before finding another relationship where jealousy doesn't have a place.

When you do, you will be so happy you did. A relationship that depends on clinging behavior isn't a relationship for the poor person who is on the receiving end of jealousy. If you can't stop yourself, question why. If it's your fault, do something about it. If it's justified bad feelings, do something about ending the relationship as it's making you into the kind of person that isn't worth being with.

The problem here is that jealousy is just a feeling. It's a suspicion and a very negative one. Look at the examples shown below. Each of them could give rise to jealousy, but it's also a good idea to read on and see where these jealous feelings go and what they turn into because they will catch up with you in the end and hurt you more than anyone else if you let them persist.

He doesn't think I am pretty enough – Your problem, not his. Learn to like yourself or he will be driven away by your moaning.

He keeps talking to other girls – The world is full of people. Expect him to talk to others. Do you talk to men in the workplace? Do you talk to male friends? It's normal behavior. Stop clinging or you will alienate him.

She keeps going out without me – Again, it's your problem. You need to find out why you are so insecure about being on your own. If she has broken any of the boundaries that you set, you can talk about it, but don't go getting overly jealous because it won't gain you any brownie points. It will make her dread coming home to your questioning.

As you can see, there is absolutely nothing positive to be gained from jealousy. I used to be jealous of my partner because of a lack of faith in who I was. He was younger than previous partners and I thought he may leave me for someone younger. However, I decided that I should celebrate being with him and gradually over the course of years, we built up a rapport and I gained self-respect. Had I voiced my insecurities in the way of showing jealousy, I am certain I would have alienated him. Instead, I worked through my insecurities and told myself that they stemmed from past relationships. Through meditation, I was able to separate past from present and begin to like who I was, instead of having boyfriends who gave me the impression I wasn't good enough. I was always good enough. The problem was that they were looking for someone different to who I was. My current partner loves who I am and with his love and support, I don't feel an ounce of jealousy and am a better person for it.

Chapter 4 – Dealing With Jealousy From Within

It's only natural for you to become jealous of someone else once in a while. It's when you become blinded by your jealousy, however, that it becomes destructive; you'll end up wasting your time wishing you have what others have, instead of appreciating who you are and what you have.

You must learn how to deal with your jealous feelings so you can build and cement trust and security around the relationship. This also makes you a better partner, having already conquered your insecurities. If it so happens you are suffering with a partner who is excessively jealous, you could work around it and ease its harmful effects by improving from within. Where you draw the line in improving your behavior really depends on you. What you choose to do (or not do) might reduce the jealousy factor's harmful effects overall, which is best achieved by reassuring your partner.

If your partner is unable to overcome jealousy, sit down and talk about it calmly and try to avoid the "Jealousy" label. Try to make it not about your partner being at fault. Generally, people who are jealous are already insecure and may see your intrusion as being negative if you do mention jealousy. Try it another way. Try to work out what behavior actually upsets your partner and try to get to the bottom of why this upsets your partner. I remember my own partner doing this. He had the patience of a saint, but once he knew where my insecurities lay, he was much more forgiving and understanding. That's what you get during a relationship. You get to know each other. You get to gain confidence, to share fears and to know each other's weaknesses as well as strengths. Then you try to find a place of compromise that suits both of you.

Jealousy From Within or From Without?

Admit that you have a real problem before you, and that it's starting to take over your life, keeping you from truly loving your partner. Jealous feelings keep you from reaching those goals, strengthening the boundaries surrounding the relationship, and becoming an improved individual overall. Here are some obvious signs that those jealous feelings are already taking the reins.

If you are currently coping with jealousy, your first question would naturally be whether or not you are a jealous person in your relationships. If so, you would need to look deep inside you, including your history and personality, to understand your situation. There are some instances where you tend to exhibit jealous behavior without good cause. These include:

- You may not really know why you do it, but you check up on your partner without provocation most of the time, even if he has not done anything to merit suspicion. Have you ever emptied his pockets and looked for things being tell-tale?

- You just can't stand looking at your partner interacting with the opposite sex. You even go to extremes convincing yourself that all those standing on the other side of the fence have one goal in their mind—that is to steal your partner away from you.

- You could be monitoring his dress habits (maybe you have heard yourself saying, "Boy, you're all dressed up fancy just to go to work!").

- You're fuming hot walking to and fro wondering where your partner has gone to if he's late for your date or late coming home.

- You listen to your partner's phone conversations. This is in spite of the absence of any unusual/suspicious behavior, and

- Many more. There are too many to address in a simple book of this nature but if your expectations of your partner are unreasonable through jealousy, you know it and you need to do something about it, because it will wreck your relationship.

The following signs also indicate that your jealousy is slowly creeping all over your soul. These points raised show how jealousy eats at who you are and this is in your everyday reactions with people. You have to see that it's you that causes these feelings and that only you can put an end to them.

- You compare yourself to friends, family, and even co-workers. And at the end of the day, you always find yourself coming up short on those comparisons. In this case, you have problems that need to be addressed. If you can't come through this kind of negativity on your own, seek help from a psychologist because feeling that you are inferior needs to be checked. It's not fair on your partner to expect your partner to find your behavior normal. It isn't.

- If ever you are jealous of someone specific, you can't bring yourself to bear hanging out with the person for a couple of minutes without wishing you had what he/she has (looks, clothes, and even the attitude). This is when jealousy really is unreasonable. What someone else looks like, what they own or who they are bears no relationship to who you are. Separate the two because while you compare, you will always come out bottom of the list. Why? Because that's where you put yourself.

- Your jealousy extends to your partner's relationship with friends and family, wishing your relationship was as good as (or much better than) theirs. Being jealous of the relationship your partner has with his/her family is about as ridiculous as it gets. They have an established relationship and you may learn something more by enjoying it, rather than being jealous of it.

- You are so obsessed that you start looking at your partner's Facebook page constantly. And it doesn't end here. You also scrutinize his emails and phone for any signs that he cheated on you. If you really are that insecure, you have problems, rather than your partner. Facebook pages can't be taken seriously. As for reading his/her email, if you are that insecure, then you don't deserve to have a partner. There has to be an element of trust or the relationship isn't worth having.

- There's also this helpless feeling of how you become incredibly jealous if your partner hangs out with new friends. Then all of a sudden you just heard yourself asking, "What is wrong with me?" What's wrong with you is that you begrudge your partner having any other relationship and that's totally unreasonable. Relationships with friends and family should be able to go side by side with your relationship with each other. If they don't then boundaries need to be set, or you will drive your partner away. Imagine trying to tell a partner to keep away from his/her family. It isn't going to happen. It's natural that his/her family form part of your life together. Get used to it.

By now you realize where you stand, and you also want to break away from that jealousy cycle and reclaim your self-control instead. You want to achieve this because you (including your partner) do not want to go crazy.

This may sound silly, but how about you start believing in your partner? Take him on his word. If he lies, then he's just making a fool out of himself—remember that. Trust is always the cornerstone of any relationship. Everything starts with trust and you have to trust in this fact for your relationship to work. Understand that doubting his word or even the decency of his behavior every time is very insulting to your partner, especially to his worth to you. It has to stop somewhere. Questioning almost everything constantly is as bad as having a secret affair in the long run.

It's only normal that the distrust lingers (probably out of habit), but you have to make an effort to act 'as if' you believe him. Presenting this 'front' will do wonders in many ways. Once you've determined that your partner is really who he is, then you have to stop right there and then. When he tells you he loves you, believe him.

This is easier said than done, but you really have to put a stop to comparing yourself to others.

Not all jealous feelings are fueled by low self-esteem. You constantly say to yourself, "I don't understand how anyone could like someone like me, or better yet, love me!" But the thing is none of us are supposed to grasp the whole idea of why someone would love us. Think about it. While you are well able to identify with and appreciate all the attractive qualities that help define you, consider this one fact—this world is full of younger, richer, better-looking, smarter, and funnier individuals. All these, though, remain as qualities, and not the whole package. If your partner loves you, it is because of those extra and indefinable qualities that he cannot, and will not, even bother to explain.

Stop asking him/her to reassure you of their love. It's the worst thing possible to have someone hanging on saying:

"Do you love me?"

"Do you think I look pretty?"

"Do you think I am good enough?"

"Do you think I am as good as ...?"

The fact is that if your partner didn't think that, he/she would not be with you. Stop second guessing yourself and let them love you. You can kill a relationship by being too needy. Think about the people in life that you avoid and why you avoid them and the chances are that they are too needy of you and you find that really hard to cope with. By being that way with your partner, you are doing exactly the same thing. Let your partner define how pretty you are in his own time. If you are a man, let your woman make you feel good about who you are instead of second guessing yourself and looking needy. People don't need the negativity and will eventually walk away from it because when you say:

"Do you really love me?"

What you are doing is questioning the authenticity of their love or their motive for being with you. Wouldn't you rather just be loved and be grateful that your partner loves who you are, warts and all? Isn't that romantic? Wouldn't you agree to just leave it that way? Anyone sitting beside you would. There will always be those intangibles in you that your partner will always relate to, and this transcends your looks, wealth, youth, and other factors. In fact, some of the well-loved individuals in history fell way below the list when talking about looks, wealth, or prestige. This should be reason enough to stop worrying why someone could possibly love you.

Chapter 5 – Be Prepared to Lose Someone

This might seem a terrible idea, but it brings a lot of sense to the table. Since low self-esteem does not trigger all of the jealous feelings we experienced, those with high self-esteem are prone to intense jealousy. This is so because they are so used to be at the center of many things. Persons with high-self esteem tend to regard other people around them as material property. It could be that they are not used to the idea of sharing their 'property', even to the point of allowing their partners to give out innocent smiles, or worse, to socialize with other people.

You know this is not you, however. You know perfectly that people are not toys or objects that need constant guarding. If you want to love someone the right way, you must be prepared for the event that you are going to lose them. This may seem mad and reckless, but it's not. Let's try and demonstrate this. Many women who are in relationships that are abusive have jealous partners who beat them. They stay with them because their self-esteem is so battered that they don't believe themselves worthy of anything better. That's not a good place to be.

Fear, anger, jealousy, and insecurity are obvious intangibles that drive love away. Love not only needs care to flourish; you also need to invest in your fearlessness. It's only normal to fear losing our partners to someone else, and eventually fear how you'll deal with the loss. But if you must continue to rely on your imagination to see things through, use it to channel your fears to whatever was the worst thing that happened to you in your past that you eventually came out of unscathed and even stronger, especially those scenarios in which you thrived.

As you work with your imagination, fantasize yourself reacting positively to the loss, thinking and believing that what doesn't kill you will only make you stronger. List down what you believe you should do to build up your life positively if your relationship won't last. Our fears are much greater if we lay our cards on table, just like you would think about what would happen if there was nothing out there for you after the relationship has ended.

If the relationship has reached the stage where the other person's jealousy is wrecking your life, you need to walk away. If it's gotten to the stage that your jealousy is wrecking their life, then it's time they walked away.

Do not build your life around the relationship alone. Do not live your life constantly asking how you would be able to live your life without your partner. Conditioning yourself that there is life after all these makes you feel good. Actually, work it out. I knew two people who were in bad relationships. One of them had such bad self-esteem issues that she didn't think she could do better, so she stayed with a partner who was abusive. However, when she did discover who she was and who she could be without him, she started to live a wonderfully successful life. Your life shouldn't stop because you are in a relationship. You should still be able to do things. You should never use a partner as a prop for your own inadequacies. That's a really foolish thing to do because it's like putting someone else in the driving seat of your life and your life is worth more than that.

Quit Playing Games...

So goes the song. Playing games around relationships just to create something by making the guy on the other side of the fence jealous is a bad idea, as jealousy can be excruciatingly uncomfortable. People normally try to get themselves to feel much better by inciting jealousy. This is achieved by flirting with others in front of your partner most of the time, or constantly claiming how someone you work with at the office is so fun, witty, and attractive. You could also go out of your way by talking about past lovers and how they didn't make you feel any better during the course of those relationships.

Of course this should not suggest that you pretend to your partner that there really are no attractive people in this world, though you could acknowledge it without having to resort to using it as your relationship ammunition. Should your partner become unfaithful to you, know that it's a reflection of him, not you. And it's also much better if he doesn't have the ammo to recoil and fire back, "Well, who's always talking about that other guy?" or "Can you blame me? You're the one who's flirting around. And you blame me?" Do not wait for the conversation to degrade into this. Ditch the game-playing tactic and keep your dignity intact.

One of the least healthy reactions to a relationship is measuring your partner. If your partner believes that he/she won't measure up to others, just playing the measuring up game could be enough to make them want to back out of the relationship. I know I would. I am not prepared to have people measure me or compare me to others. If a partner of mind decided to play that game, I already know my value and if they don't, then tough! I certainly wouldn't play the game with them and would prefer to end a relationship than to live with someone who plays head games.

Make-Believe is Different from Reality

Like many existing psychological problems (hypochondria, paranoia, etc.) people experience, jealousy is driven by our imaginations running amok. Imagination is a good thing—if you channel it through positively. It becomes bad once it starts messing with your head. Certain individuals draw on their imaginations to think and do good things. Stephen King, with his stellar career of making things up and writing them down for everyone to enjoy, is a great example.

What makes him stand out is not the quality and intensity of his imagination, but rather his way of distancing himself from all the stuff coming out of his head. He clearly knows that whatever he writes is not real because of how he sees it. Drifting towards the make-believe is destructive in all relationships. Just think about what your imagination will play into your head when your partner comes home unusually late from work, for example.

- You begin to imagine him having a leisurely drink with someone you saw in his workplace one time.

- You become upset, angry, and frightened—that without any evidence in your hands your imagination might be real after all. And it goes on further.

- By now, your imagination starts chanting the 'what ifs'. And if you dance to that tune, then your mind will suddenly be filled with so many negative things that shouldn't be there in the first place.

You can only imagine where your imagination will take you. If you make an effort to stop getting all emotional and crazy just because your jealousy played you using your imagination, then you'll come out strong. You'll also come out one step closer to regaining the upper hand with your all your jealous tendencies.

Use your imagination positively instead and you'll feel better, not worse. Close your eyes, ease your mind, and think of nothing else. Now imagine the scenario that brings out your jealous feelings. Is the scenario about your partner going out and being all smiles with someone else? Do you see your partner chatting and laughing with another person?

After making out such scenarios, start some deep breathing. Imagine yourself slowly looking focused and calm at the same time, showing no interest whatsoever in the scenario in front of you. This should encourage you to believe that, ultimately, you only have yourself to answer to, and no one else. Only you can truly control yourself. Many have approved how this path is more productive than dealing with the issue head on in a reckless sense.

Think about how your partner made you jealous; act on it by responding with a rather calm detachment, instead of fueling your jealousy. The more you do this (and become comfortable with this), the less your life will be shrouded in jealousy.

I actually used the extra time that my boyfriend left me with because of being home later from work to my benefit. It's extra time to do the things you want to do. It's extra time to actually have time to yourself to enjoy. Stop seeing it as negative. If you want his approval and you want his attention, enjoy your time on your own and when he/she comes into your day, be happy to share that part of the day with your loved one. Imagine this case scenario.

- A guy works late because his boss expects it of him.

- His girlfriend assumes he has a mistress.

- She confronts him with this news.

- Turns out he was working late to try and buy her a birthday present.

In a case such as this, all that is left is regret. He will regret ever wanting to buy her anything nice. She will regret opening her mouth and voicing her opinion. Now try this scenario:

- He works later than normal

- She prepares a super supper for him

- He comes home and they make love in front of the fire

He appreciates her because she works hard too. She appreciates him because she knows how hard he has to work. He wants to come home because she's positive, lively and loves him. She gets great satisfaction from the situation because she knows that he doesn't want anyone else. If you start to put restrictions onto relationships, you actually stifle them and even the strongest of relationships may not be able to survive jealousy.

Lengthen the Leash

Don't tighten it (dog reference here). Relax! Watch a movie; let things flow on their course. Lengthen the leash. If your partner plans on spending the weekend with friends, let him go and have fun. If you tighten the leash in the hopes that he won't be able to anything to hurt the relationship, then you'll be living in an unhealthy relationship in the long run. To 'imprison' your partner will only fuel his desire to free himself from your possessiveness. Give him freedom to have fun and spend time with friends and he'll believe, without a doubt, that this is a great relationship to be in.

I learned this when my own partner wanted to go on a trip with his friends. We had not been apart before and it seemed a very strange request. Thinking about it, I actually worked out that I could do all the girly things that were important to me if he wasn't there and by being cheerful about his trip, he actually told me that he was so happy that I felt that way. We retain our character by allowing ourselves to remain individuals even though in a relationship. That's very healthy indeed. Trust is what it's all about and if trust isn't there, then the big green monster starts to examine things and comes up with scenarios that probably don't exist anyway. If my husband wanted to leave me, then denying him the chance of that trip away wouldn't do me anyway because he would still leave. Why imprison your man? When you lengthen the leash, you are giving him a clear message that the relationship is built on trust. When you get in the way of your partner's person freedom because of jealous thoughts, you may just be cutting your own lifeline.

The other thing to think about is that you are two separate individuals. Why go on vacation with him if your interests are different to his? Why suffer two weeks of going around museums when you hate museums? Why make him sit on a beach when he hates even putting on his shorts?

If you can get beyond jealous thoughts, you can find a really nice place to be. It gives you independence within the framework of a relationship and that makes your relationship even more valuable because you have more to share with each other after the event.

Quite often, jealousy means that your partner can't fulfill ambitions. Your partner can't go on vacation alone because you won't let him/her. If you begin to stifle your partner's dreams, expect him/her to be bitter because no one should have their dreams put on a backburner simply because of a jealous wife/husband/girlfriend or boyfriend. It's unreasonable.

You may have forgotten the biggest fact of them all. You get one chance at this life and if you choose to screw it up with jealousy, you may actually never get a chance to make amends to your partner. Your partner may just grab his/her own dreams and leave you and your jealousy to fester.

Chapter 6 – Making a Connection Brings a Cure to Your Jealousy

Open up. As jealousy strikes women, they begin to question themselves about whether they're pretty enough, or smart enough to attract and keep men's (or rather a specific individual's) attention. Keeping a healthy body, mind, and spirit paves the way for building up self-esteem that enables us to answer such questions with a Yes in all honest—"Yes, I am great and I am worthy of love and a fulfilling relationship that is based on honesty and trust." And believe it or not, THAT is really what men are looking for in women these days. Of course, physical looks may already be a given requisite (blame it on their fantasies) but it's who you are inside that attracts them the most.

Furthermore, various physical activities release chemicals (enter the endorphins) that, among other known benefits, give your self-esteem that needed boost. So, whatever you do, always connect and communicate with your partner.

Making a connection also needs a solid foundation. This means working things out on your part, like following your passions, pursuing hobbies, or getting into sports and other leisure activities. This would also be a good time to reconnect with family and friends, catching up on lost time and strengthening the bonds. All these also set the stage so you could pamper yourself. You'll be surprised that you are not comparing yourself to other women anymore.

Bring Out Your Secret Weapon

It's no secret, but your confidence in yourself is what wins the day, and men believe self-confidence is sexy.

Note that showing trust, respect, and love to your man, complemented by your easy-going personality (this you have to build up after realizing that jealousy is not really for you), has more power over your obsessive jealousy when it comes to his decision to stay faithful to you. If you are able to control your jealous feelings and showcase your true beauty instead, he'll have all the reasons to remain faithful to you. He'll also become impartial to other women's attention as well.

Time to Stop Feeding the Green-Eyed Monster

Understand that whatever you do, and no matter how much effort you put into it, your jealous feelings will be there for a while. Jealousy is not something you can just command to go away overnight.

It's perfectly normal. Besides, after seeing the bigger picture, it's not really the problem. It's the toll taken on your self-esteem and self-worth, and the feelings of security that you have to face now. But rest easy. All these feelings will eventually ease down on you—that is, if you stop feeding that lurking monster.

Since communication in the relationship is a must to keep the monster at bay, you now need to connect with your partner and talk to him in a positive mood. As already mentioned above, how you communicate to your partner regarding this issue really matters. You would not want one small misconception to ruin it all, would you?

Talk to your partner about the jealousy issue so both of you can manage and prevent it, not dwell on it further. Share with him what you feel without hurling any accusations. Make your requests crystal clear—"I don't know, but I think I'm beginning to feel a bit insecure." This would be a good, positive approach. "It'd be better if we finalize our plans so we can both look forward to spending time together."

It's Much Better This Way, Would You Agree?

See to it that you request specific things with the aim of containing your insecurities (or to prevent starting one), like planning the calls that you guys will be making to each other, or taking the time to share experiences of the day. The better the connection between the two of you the lesser the instances of jealousy surfacing in the relationship.

Managing Your Stress at the Same Time

Another way of seeing jealousy is in its nature as being a stress response. This implies that, once you're feeling anxious and overwhelmed, your jealousy becomes more intense, like something very heavy inside your chest, and you'll have to carry it wherever you go. Before you look for reassurance from your partner, make sure you have already done your part; manage your anxiety by engaging your heart and mind in a healthy lifestyle change (good nutrition, exercise and meditation/yoga) and a whole lot of support surrounding you. Whenever you are in a self-care mode, the green-eyed monster tends to settle down.

Know That You Are One Lucky Person

It's now high time that you remind yourself that fortune favors you. Back then, when you were still blinded with jealousy, not only did you find it impossible to see everything objectively and with clarity, you had trouble realizing just how fortunate you are for being the person that you are right now. You are lucky because you are living a good life, enjoying great food, exploring other places, and having fun with friends and family whenever you feel like it. Just take a look at others who are not fortunate enough to have what you possess right now and you'll see. Know that you possess so many things (not to mention your uniqueness as an individual) that other people would envy and be jealous of.

This is all intended to help you with your relationship jealousy, but relationship jealousy doesn't stop there. It's a very complex thing. In the next section we deal with behaviors or past events that may lead to jealousy and show you how to overcome those feelings. These could have arisen because of circumstances, or they could have arisen simply because you have ideas set in your mind about what should happen, what did happen and why you feel this way.

There are many examples of where siblings feel jealousy for one another and even more where friendships are lost to jealousy. Jealousy of possessions or chances in life may be excuses for the individual. Instead of asking themselves why it's possible for someone to have something, they tend to ask themselves why they are not getting what they deserve. That creates jealousy and it's very unhealthy to picture life in this way.

In the following chapters, we look at how your childhood affects your level of jealousy and how you can overcome this. We also look at relationships which were unacceptable and which lead to insecurities that may make you feel unreasonably jealous now.

Then, lastly, we look at strengthening your character so that jealousy becomes a thing of the past rather than an everyday feeling you and the people around you have to ensure as a result of knowing each other. Jealousy isn't healthy. It's negative and it fuels all kinds of negative feelings within a relationship or even within yourself. You need to rid yourself of it because what it's doing is eating away at your own sense of self-worth and your worth to others. Others may view you are being "toxic" or too needy and that's not a good reflection on you at all. If you get this reputation, you will lose friends and you won't be able to keep a lover because no one wants toxic relationships and no one wants someone whose needs are so great that they upset the balance of the relationship.

Chapter 7 – Jealousy Caused by Inadequacy

As you grow up, you are influenced by things that happen in your life. Your parents may compare you with a sibling. That comparison may not be something that the sibling enjoys any more than you do and it's certainly not fair that parents should compare one child negatively to another. This will cause jealousy from an early age and if you feel any kind of jealousy toward a sibling, it can last a lifetime. These are phrases that may be familiar to you:

- "Why can't you behave yourself like your sister does?"

- "Why don't you have the common sense of your brother?"

- "Why are you so stupid?

Unfortunately, when people become parents, there is no handbook. There will be moments when parents find that they are out of their depths with despair. One child acts up, another doesn't. One child seems normal and has loads of friends, the other is withdrawn. One child studies hard – another finds it hard to read even the simplest of words. Of course, in circumstances such as this, parents don't know what to do. They worry for their kids, but they are out of their depths because these are not behavioral experts. In a moment of frustration, they use comparisons because they don't know any other way of explaining to their kids what's wrong. In the process, though, they can do much harm to the psyche of a child.

The child may think that he/she doesn't measure up. The child may see one sibling as always being favored and this makes that child feel deprived of something. The child may also feel that a parent doesn't love him/her. These are all typical patterns that can happen in childhood. The green eyed monster can start even at the age of 2 when a child's toy is snatched from him by a parent and given to another child to play with. It's serious stuff for the child and he remembers that negative feeling that someone got the best out of the situation and that he was left feeling betrayed.

Jealousy can take the form of feeling inferior to a sibling. It may be something that happens when a child feels that a sibling is better looking, more intelligent or better treated by the parents. The child sees this as unjust and perhaps it is, but the point is that if you continue to make comparisons all of your life, there will always be the haves and the have-nots, the pretty and the plain, the fat and the slim, the rich and the poor. The comparisons that people have in their lives will always be there and while it's quite healthy to work toward presenting yourself in the best way possible, it's not healthy to feel jealous or envious of those who have what it is that you want.

Finding a New Way Forward

It may be a good idea to write down your negative feelings about others to fully understand them. Some will be jealousies that are caused because you don't measure up to them in some way and these are the ones that you need to look at. It's not possible for you to be them. You need to just be happy with who you are and stop chasing rainbows by seeing what they have as being better than you have. It's unreasonable. It's even insulting to them that you have a fixation about something they have no control over. That's really childish and shows a real lack of self-esteem.

"She has prettier hair than me – she can afford the stylist. I can't."

Look how negative this statement is and it provokes jealousy. You want hair like hers but you can't afford the styling – so instead of feeling bad about something she has that you can't have, find a way that you can have it. If this means going out and earning more and saving toward it, that works. Alternatively, you could enlist her help and ask advice on how you can do your hair that would look like that. The point is she knows what it takes and may be able to come up with cheaper alternatives that give you the same looks. Stop blaming her for having something you haven't got. It's not her fault. It's yours for perceiving it in that way. If you are not happy about your looks, alter them. Try different styles and see what you can come up with that suits you. The answer lies with you, not with her and being jealous of her serves no one, least of all you. It makes you look childish and it makes her feel bad that you have such a negative fixation about her looks.

"He is way too intelligent for me."

You cannot be jealous about things that are just what they are. There are people who are more intelligent. There always will be. The brain surgeon may be more intelligent than the nurse who deals with the day to day needs of patients. The chief of the hospital may be more intelligent than the surgeon. It takes all of these people to make the hospital work like it does. That means that, no matter what your level of intelligence, you have a place in life and need to find it and be happy with it, instead of feeling jealous about people who are more intelligent than you.

"He never acknowledges me when we are out in public."

If you find yourself ignored by your partner in public, it's probably because you haven't shown him/her the best side of your personality. You need to watch people. See how people behave in public. If you are the jealous type, why he is avoiding you is because he doesn't want to see the look of disapproval every time the poor guy talks to someone of the opposite sex.

He doesn't want to see your miserable response to his behavior. He doesn't acknowledge you because you don't acknowledge his right to be himself. That's not fair. If you have a problem with your partner, talk about it openly and not just from your angle. Your angle may just be skewed by bad experiences in the past. Instead of criticizing, try talking and help him to protect you more from feeling jealousy because if he understands the past experience that made you feel so bad, he will want to help you to get over it and move on in a more positive way.

If you feel inadequate in some way, or have self-esteem issues, whether these are high self-esteem that expects too much of others all the time, or low self-esteem that expects nothing and usually gets nothing, you do need to work on self-esteem because as long as you see yourself on a different level to people around you, this will always be a cause for jealousy and discontent. Forget trying to be sorry for yourself. You have the same opportunities as anyone else. Stop using your own sense of inadequacy as a reason to be jealous because its negativity will eventually lose you all of the friendships you have.

Put yourself in a room on your own. Think about whether you are a happy person. If you are not, write down the things that make you unhappy. It is these things that will lead you to unleashing happiness because once they are addressed, you find that the little green monster inside you gets tamed so that his presence is barely noticeable anymore and that's when you really win and your partner is likely to win as well. Then, you will gain friends and be a better friend to the people that you know. Jealousy kills friendships. It kills the inner you and makes you worth less to the people who surround you. Let go of jealousy and you free yourself of a negative influence that can ruin your life.

Chapter 8 – Learn to Love Yourself

People often see a statement like this and think in terms of the "Love and Peace" generation of the sixties. They see it as unrealistic and a little too corny to actually be of use. However, it really does work and you need to understand why. If you love yourself or at least are happy with the person that you are, you stop being so clinging and you lose the need to be jealous. My best friend has a better car than me, she has a better house, a more reliable husband, but she's my best friend because none of this counts. It's her personality, stability and her love of life that makes her my best friend. In fact, once upon a time, she admitted to feeling a little jealous of me and that shocked me. I asked her why because from where I was standing, I didn't have anything she couldn't have. I was no one special and I was pretty poor. What she said demonstrated something fundamental to relationships.

"You are so happy in yourself," was her reply. When I examined this, I found that her life was quite complex even though it seemed to me that she had everything a person could ever want. She loved life and she seemed very stable in her attitude toward everyone and I loved her as a friend, but what didn't she have and what could actually have made her jealous? She didn't have time for her. Her commitments in life left her very little time for herself. That's what she was jealous of but it wasn't a real jealousy that bites into a relationship. It was a yen on her part to experience that freedom.

When we talked about it, it seemed that although she was happy in her life and didn't seem to have any problems, she was depriving herself of time that she needed for her. We talked about it for a long time, and we worked out that she needed to reschedule her life a little bit so that an hour here and an hour there allowed her all the time that she needed. Her problem was that although she liked who she was, she always put other people in front of her when it came to allocating time within her life. It wasn't a huge jealousy on her part, but when she saw that it was her that was causing her problem, she was able to put it right. If you don't love yourself equally to others, you tend to put yourself last and when you do that for any length of time, it can cause you a great deal of negativity, self-esteem issues and resentment that leads to jealousy.

Loving yourself doesn't mean ignoring everybody else's needs. It just means knowing the importance of your own needs and fitting them into your life. These make you feel more fulfilled and happier about your life and less inclined to feel any kind of jealousy. If someone has something emotionally that you don't have then the only place you can find it is inside yourself and that's what self-love is all about. It's a case of knowing priorities that lead you to feeling fulfilled.

Exercise in Loving Yourself

Try to think of an experience in life that made you really happy and fulfilled. It could be a place, an experience from childhood, but it must be a warm and happy memory. Close your eyes and concentrate on it. Feel it creep over you. Feel the warmth of it and enjoy it. Let this be your private space where you go when you feel negative feelings toward other people. Instead of reacting with jealousy, simply distance yourself from the situation and sit down and close your eyes, visiting that place of comfort for a little while.

This form of meditation can help you because it lessens the chances of you turning a bad situation into a worse one by demonstrating jealousy. You can do this anywhere at any time and even if you need to escape to the Lady's room to do it, that's as good a place as any. Give yourself calm and that calm will help you to walk back into the situation with a calmer mind that is able to see the situation logically, rather than letting your emotional mind take over.

It's a good idea to also get accustomed to using relaxation exercises to help to regenerate the way that you think. People who are up tight and jealous tend to be people who don't relax much. Instead of relaxing, they let thoughts upon thought pile up in their minds so that situations become even more difficult than they need to be. Jealousy which is allowed to fester and then manifest itself is one of the most destructive feelings in the world, and if you can step away from the potential of doing that, you may find that you love yourself more and feel more loved by others.

Loving yourself means being the kind of person you are okay with. You are happy in your own company and you don't leech off others to try and find your balance in life. If you cannot stand being alone, then you need to find that balance and if this means practicing meditation or going into that joyful place occasionally that you can conjure up in your mind, you will be a better person for doing that.

Chapter 9 – Turning the Tables to See the Reality

Have you ever imagined what jealousy feels like on the receiving end? The chances are that it hasn't crossed your mind. You are jealous and you are too pre-occupied with the injustices that are being done to you to actually look from another person's viewpoint. Imagine yourself in his/her shoes and reverse your jealous feelings and aim them toward yourself, because you may be shocked at the way that these feelings make you feel.

Jealousy with Your Partner

You think he is unfaithful? Okay, let's put the shoe on the other foot and imagine how you would feel if he thought and said the same about you. You would probably be outraged. You would probably be angry especially if you had never even thought of being unfaithful and yet here is the person that you trust the most in life and who you have chosen for a partner accusing you of infidelity. Although you may not be able to do this at first, it's worth following the pattern shown below to get you over being jealous, because a jealous person is not a very attractive potential for a partner.

- Think jealous thought

- Reverse it to aim it at you

- Know how it makes you feel

- Approach the subject in another way

Accusing someone of being unfaithful alienates them, especially if it isn't true. If it is true, what do you gain by being jealous?

This makes your partner more likely to stray because he/she wants to get away from that stifling feeling of being in an environment which is hostile. Believe it, jealousy causes hostility. If your partner is working long hours, appreciate him/her when he/she comes home from work. Make the situation at home so agreeable that your partner will want to be at home. Even if it is found that your partner has strayed, jealousy serves no purpose. Your partner will already feel guilt and you will already feel betrayed. What point is there to prolonging the bad feeling by letting jealousy take a part in an already negative situation?

Chapter 10 – Jealousy among Siblings

This was a subject that came up when my family gathered after the death of a relative. We had not seen each other for years and my siblings sat down and talked quite a bit during the arranging of the funeral. What transpired was very interesting indeed. People carry negativity through their lives from childhood. Some manage to get beyond that negativity. For others, it sticks and it's very destructive indeed to the relationship between siblings and it may all be totally unnecessary.

For instance, I always thought my sister was the favorite. It turned out that she always thought I was. She told me how, as the eldest, she was always pushed harder. She had a mother and father who had never parented before and so they read all the books and pushed her in directions which were not always easy for her. She succeeded in life, but she always had this jealousy in her mind for her younger sisters. I asked why. It didn't seem to make sense, and what transpired was that she thought that the younger kids had experienced an easier time of it because our parents were more experienced as parents and didn't push the younger ones so much. It's an interesting situation because each child carried jealousy with them through adulthood and had these misconceptions about life as it was. Every single person sees life through their individual viewpoint. I saw my life as being lived in her shadow. She saw her life as being harder and remembered leaving home because she couldn't stand it anymore.

Often you need to reverse the jealousy to make sense of it. If you feel jealous of a sibling for being more talented than you are, imagine how you would feel in her shoes. She is talented so everyone expects more of her. To add to that, she has jealous brothers and sisters who throw negative vibes in her direction. That's not very fair is it?

Now imagine, your brother wins the affection of someone you like. This could be a friend who you are now forced to see less because of your brother's attention to her. It could be someone you fancied but never had the courage to ask out. Jealousy in a situation such as this makes the situation worse. You feel:

"He is taking away my friend." Or "He has taken away my chances."

The fact of the matter is that your sibling has simply gone on and done something in his life that you see as affecting you. He didn't do it to bug you. He didn't do it because he doesn't love you. He did it because opportunity opened the door and he entered. Now imagine yourself in his place when you start to criticize:

- "You spend too much time with her and not enough with me."

- "You only asked her out because you knew I wanted to."

The problem is that jealous people believe the world revolves around them. They don't see beyond that. If you did accuse your brother of either of these, you would alienate him even further and that's even more destructive and gets a worse result because the likelihood is that your jealousy will put more distance between you and helps no one.

There are always consequences to jealousy. You make yourself feel even less important than you are and become wretched in your thoughts. If you voice the jealousy, you then have to live with all the regrets of what you said and become smaller in the mind of the person that you criticized.

For the person who has jealousy aimed at them, there are also consequences. They feel stifled. They feel that you are trying to push them into a corner where you want them and will resist that because it's a natural feeling to want to reject that kind of behavior. Jealousy is completely counter-productive to any relationship.

It really is time for you to understand what it feels like when someone is jealous. If you find jealous feelings coming into your mind, imagine your friend or lover saying what you feel to you and understand that there are consequences and that these are always negative.

Chapter 11 – Observing Healthy Relationships

You can learn an awful lot from examining relationships around you. For example, if a couple seem happy, look at the way that they interact together. It's unlikely that either one of them acts in a mean way. In fact, they probably harmonize very well with each other. Their work life home life balance will be carefully worked out. They will spend time together and chances are that they share a lot of things in common. Observing people helps you to work out what you are doing wrong.

Asking for Help

When you know someone that has a happy and stable relationship, this is probably the best kind of person to talk to about any doubts that you have. If you want to ask for help, be considerate. Remember that other people have busy lives and if you need in depth conversation, make sure that you choose a time that suits them when they can give you the time you need. A good approach may be to telephone and ask if they can spare you a little time to help you with something. Good friends are always willing to help you but don't abuse that privilege. This isn't a time when you can spend valuable moments criticizing your partner. This isn't what it's about. It's about you.

Try to tell them about your insecurity. Try to explain the predicament that you find yourself in and explain how you are finding it hard to get away from feeling jealousy but that you want to. The fact that you have owned up to having a problem will alert them to the fact that you are serious and want their advice. If you approach it in another manner, what may happen is that your friend may misunderstand your need. Let's show you what the conversation should **not** be like:

"I think Chuck is being unfaithful." – This isn't what it's about. It makes your friend alienated toward Chuck and they may even fire up your jealousy even more by adding to it. That's not going to help anyone at all.

"I have a problem and I really need your help." – This is a better approach because you have taken ownership of the problem. When you go on to discuss your jealousy, instead of using the first phrase in this section which blames Chuck, you need to open a more effective dialog that blames no one.

"You are a good friend of mind. You know what I am like. I can't control feelings of jealousy."

That's an honest approach and your friend may be able to talk you around into having more confidence in yourself or may suggest that you perhaps need to talk to a professional to try and get over the jealousy issue. She may even have something to contribute that makes you feel better about the situation and help you to overcome the feelings of jealousy without letting them destroy your relationship. Good friends tend to help to pull you out of your funky moods and she may be willing to talk you through your problems or search into why you feel so insecure.

Learn from people who don't display jealousy. If you are a teen, for example, and you confide in someone you know to be jealous of others, they fuel your jealousy even further and make it the focal point in your life. Don't discuss it with negative people because they are likely to make your situation worse. Observe people who are happy within their lives because these are people who have all of their priorities worked out and are much more likely to help you to sort out your problems.

Healthy relationships in general depend upon give and take and sometimes you can engineer situations which improve your self-worth. Bake a cake for a neighbor just for the sake of it and make a very old lady happy. Do things for others that give you a better sense of who you are. People who love you do so because they see this positive side of your nature which endears them to you. When that's overshadowed by jealousy, it takes away the joy of the relationship and makes it very negative indeed. Try to do things which give you back your self-worth. Make a conscious effort to be a positive person and to follow the example of positive people you know who are in successful relationships.

If you feel jealous, it's not another person's fault. The fault lies with you. You can't change what other people do or what they have. You can have a positive impact on people if you drop jealousy and decide you are worth more than that.

Chapter 12 – Getting Beyond Your Fears

Often people who are jealous have fears. They fear losing what is dear to them. They fear not measuring up, when no one is actually measuring them. They go to extreme lengths with their relationships because of the fears that they hold. For example, I knew one couple and the husband would not allow his wife to talk to males. There was no question of her doing that because it was made clear at the beginning of the relationship that he didn't accept that kind of behavior. What happened from then on was that things went from bad to worse.

She was not allowed to look at other people in restaurants. She wasn't allowed to telephone anyone male and that included a family friend in their nineties! If that isn't irrational enough, she was accused of having an affair if she was seen looking at another male when she was out shopping. It all boiled down to a lack of self-confidence and fear of losing the relationship, which were very real fears indeed. Instead of trying to find out why those fears were dominating his life, the man continued to hound his wife with his jealous questions until she couldn't take any more and did the very thing that he feared the most – she left.

What killed the relationship?

Jealousy killed the relationship and it has been guilty of killing millions of relationships since time began. People cannot live a life where they feel there is no trust, there is no room to breathe and they feel like they are being suffocated. Unfortunately, jealous people do just that. They hold onto their belief about how the relationship should be manifested and when their partner doesn't react in a way that they expect, jealousy kicks in.

Reducing Fears in the Relationship

While you cannot take away all of your fears in life, you can minimize them. Talk about what you expect out of the relationship and see that it's on course with what they want. Talk about where you want the relationship to go and be straightforward about it. Learn to trust. Love can't be a real thing if there's no trust involved. This is a two way street and for a relationship to succeed, there has to be a level of trust. Talk about your hopes and dreams. Talk about your fears and let your partner assure you and give you the confidence needed to gain that trust. It takes time to develop a relationship. Don't jump in with both feet unless you and your partner are willing to take that commitment. Otherwise, you are heading for disaster. If it's your dream but it's not your partner's dream, it won't work but if you are able to share your dreams and both be aiming in the same direction, this helps you to take away a lot of the fears that you may otherwise have expressed in jealousy.

You need to be complete as a human being before you enter a relationship because this jealousy thing isn't about anyone else. It's about you. If you enter into a relationship without first having learned to comfortably accept who you are and be happy with that person you have turned out to be, you will never find happiness with someone else. Insecurities in yourself will always surface, no matter how much your partner loves you, because they are part of who you are. Resolving those problems takes a little bit of time and that means time on your own. Get used to who you are. Like who you are and don't always bend to the will of someone else. A partnership has to be a two way thing, but before you can even enter one, you need to be a whole human being – rather than a broken one.

If old relationships have left you broken, you need time to heal and mend. Jealousy can easily creep into your life if you already have fears about who you are. I see it time and time again and there's nothing that anyone can do about it. Friends make mistakes, relationships fall apart but those that fall apart because of jealousy do so because jealous people are incomplete people.

Have you ever heard the expression from one partner to another that he or she isn't complete without their partner? It's actually not that true. They may feel life isn't as satisfying and may miss their partner terribly if something happens, but if you go into a relationship and need it to the extent that you can't exist without the other person, you are not yet ready for a relationship. It's not fair on them and it's stupidity on your part to believe that another person makes you whole. Learn to cope with your fears. Learn to live with them and learn to like yourself because everybody has the potential to have fears which are unresolved, but while they are unresolved, life won't work like it should. That's when jealousy starts to raise its ugly head.

If you need help getting beyond jealousy and find that it takes up all of your thoughts and you are unable to resolve these thoughts by yourself, it may be beneficial to talk to a counsellor who can help you to understand where all of that jealousy is coming from. It's very unhealthy and it helps no one to feel that way. With the help of a counsellor, you will be able to see why you feel so jealous and work your way through it. In fact, if jealousy is taking over your life and you can't resolve it, this may be the most permanent way to face up to your fears, to grab them by the hand and face up to them, knowing that the professional is there for you and will work through those fears with you. Sometimes, you can't do it alone, but you do need to face up to whatever fears are wrecking your trust in others, because you can't build a relationship based on jealous thoughts.

The benefits of getting beyond jealousy:

- You feel more confidence in yourself and others

- You learn to use your instincts to trust people

- Your relationships will last longer

- You won't alienate friends

On the other hand, you can look at the disadvantages and decide whether you want to live with all of these limitations getting in the way of your happiness. At the end of the day, you do have a choice. If you have unresolved problems that cause you to feel jealous, it's time to sort them out, leave them behind you and begin to live your life in a way that is more enriched and based on trust. Here are the disadvantages of jealousy.

- It causes friction in a relationship

- It puts you through a lot of mental torture

- It may actually not be justified

- Its negative nature will kill relationships

- You will become someone people don't have time for

- You will break your relationship if you bring jealousy into the frame

Jealousy of others, jealousy which is unfounded and which is misplaced will spell the end of a relationship and it's not worth it. If you doubt something your partner says, learn to communicate in a positive way and you can find answers together. Looking through the eyes of jealousy really won't win you are brownie points and you will make yourself thoroughly miserable in the process.

Chapter 13 – What Famous People Say about Jealousy

You may wonder why I included this at the end of the book, but it's because it's all food for thought. There are so many quotations on jealousy that may make you think that your situation really does need examination and dissection and that until you do face your demons, you will have to face the negativity you choose to live with by being jealous.

"The jealous are troublesome to others, but torture to themselves." William Penn.

He has quite accurately described the fact that jealousy is more of a problem to you than it is to others, who may be irritated by it. The word "torture" was very purposefully used to show you just how serious this problem is. Jealousy is torture for the soul who indulges in it. If you find yourself looking at someone else's life and becoming negatively jealous because you don't have what they have, snap out of it, because you are torturing yourself. You can have what others have, but you need to visualize and plan your life so that all the good things happen for you. Jealousy is counter-productive and holds you back from ever achieving anything.

"You can be the moon and still be jealous of the stars." – Gary Allen

This quote caught my eyes because too many people are the kind of people who can shine out to others but don't see it. You may have the opportunity to be everything to someone, but you miss the mark by looking at others and comparing your lot with theirs, instead of enjoying the joy that is you. If you find yourself doing this, jealousy is the reason. It takes a wonderful human being and makes them very small indeed, until they forget who they really are. Don't let jealousy do this to you. Your grass may not look as green as your neighbors grass, but the problem may be simple. Perhaps yours just needs a little feeding.

"Jealousy is the fear of comparison." – Max Frische

This last quotation is one that you should always remember. At the bottom of the mind when jealousy is exercised is the fear of comparison. Is she prettier than me? Is he better looking than me? What can she give you that I cannot? Why does she get away with it when I don't?

Comparison is not only evil, but it causes all kinds of rifts. It is great if you have a role model that you want to emulate, but if you are always measuring yourself against people to try and find emotional answers to your unfathomable questions, you are looking in the wrong place. Comparison won't do it. Jealous people, compared with people who are not jealous are better people to trust and to welcome into your life. Thus, drop the jealousy and be a person that doesn't compare. Everyone is individual and comparison serves no purpose.

"It is not love that is blind, but jealousy." – Gerald Durrell.

This is so true that you need to remember it. Jealousy is blind to what's really going on. It's blind to someone's good side. It's blind to potential circumstance and it prefers to feed those that feel it with total negativity. Blindness caused by a lack of trust isn't something to be proud of. Stop looking for reasons, for explanations and for justifications. Close your eyes to doubt and embrace the good. There is not one single human being on the earth who is flawless. When you take the most innocent of people, you can find something they did wrong if your jealousy allows you to look far enough, but why should you? The point is that people who are unsure of themselves do go to ridiculous lengths to prove that someone has betrayed them, but in the process of feeling jealousy, they also betray themselves.

These are some great quotes used for the purpose of helping you to see the futility of jealousy. It comes on a par with hate. Hate is a very strong word and extremely negative and jealousy easily comes into the same scale of negativity because it lays a foundation for doubt. That's never something worth holding onto. When you begin to see the negative connotations of envy, and stop letting them rule your life, life becomes a much better place to be and the people around you accept you for who you are.

Conclusion

Thank you again for downloading this book! I sincerely hope that you received value from it.

I hope this book was able to help you understand why jealousy affects you and your relationship. With what you learned, you should now be able to address it and not let it drive your life around.

Finally, if you enjoyed this book, then I'd like to ask you for a favor, would you be kind enough to leave a review for this book on Amazon? I want to reach as many people as I can with this book and more reviews will help me accomplish that!

Thank you and good luck!

11544154R00050

Printed in Great Britain
by Amazon.co.uk, Ltd.,
Marston Gate.